Compassionate Communication

Mindful Conflict Resolution

Table of Contents

Chapter 1. Introduction

Welcome to a journey filled with empathy, understanding, and harmony! Our Special Report on "Compassionate Communication: Mindful Conflict Resolution" offers an enlightening exploration of a communication paradigm that can transform interactions, build solid connections, and resolve conflicts effectively. Discover the art of empathetic listening, respectful expression, and mindful mediation that can bring a sea of positive change in personal relationships, workplace dynamics, and social cooperation. This easy to comprehend report, laced with real-life examples and practical techniques, will not just enhance your communication but also enrich your life experiences. Invest in this journey to create a more compassionate world together - one conversation at a time!

Chapter 2. Understanding Compassionate Communication

Compassionate communication, sometimes referred to as nonviolent communication (NVC), was developed by psychologist Marshall Rosenberg in the 1960s. This communication strategy, at its core, fosters understanding, empathy, and harmonious coexistence. It pushes us to put ourselves in another's shoes and aims at fostering a productive, kind, and respectful conversation instead of escalating conflicts.

It's crucial to recognize compassionate communication as an art that requires practice to master. Therefore, let us untangle its key elements and explore how you can apply them in your everyday interactions.

2.1. The Underpinning Philosophy

The foundation of compassionate communication lies in an empathetic approach that involves understanding the feelings and needs of both yourself and others. This is not about being nice at the expense of your feelings, nor about sacrificing your needs for others. Instead, it views everyone as having an equal right to their feelings and needs, aiming for everyone's needs to be met, not to the detriment of others.

Compassionate communication views all human actions as attempts to meet underlying needs, even when these actions may appear harmful or disconnected. Instead of labeling the behavior as 'bad' or 'wrong', compassionate communication seeks to understand what unmet needs created the behavior.

2.2. The Four Components of Compassionate Communication

Compassionate communication comprises four distinct yet interconnected components that come together to create effective dialogue.

1. **Observation**: This is the starting point, where you state what you observe in a neutral way, not including judgments or assumptions. For example, rather than saying, "You're always late!" (which is judgmental), you might say, "I noticed you arrived 15 minutes after our agreed time" (which is neutral).

2. **Feeling**: The next step is to express how the observation makes you feel. It's crucial to distinguish between feeling and thinking, as it might be tempting to say, "I feel that you are disrespectful", which is more of an assessment than a feeling. Instead, you could say, "I feel upset."

3. **Need**: After expressing feelings, you then identify the need or value that is connected to your feeling. For instance, "I feel upset because I need respect for my time."

4. **Request**: Finally, you make a concrete request to address the need you identified. It's essential to express this as a request, not a demand. An example could be, "Could we agree on being punctual for future meetings?" Here, the focus is not on what you want the other person to stop doing but what you want them to start or continue doing.

Together, these steps form a full process that encapsulates the essence of compassionate communication.

2.3. The Language of Compassion

The language we use while practicing compassionate communication plays a critical role. There are several aspects we must consider:

1. **Judgement-free Language**: Avoid making moral judgments. Instead, focus on observations and feelings. Judgmental language creates defensiveness and counterattack, while observations promote understanding and dialog.

2. **Don't generalize**: Avoid words that generalize, like 'always' or 'never'. These statements can easily escalate conflicts as they're often exaggerations that provoke defensiveness.

3. **Personal Responsibility Language**: Use 'I' statements, expressing feelings and needs from your personal perspective. This takes responsibility for your own emotions and prevents from blaming others.

4. **Empathetic Listening**: This involves fully focusing on the speaker's feelings and needs. Guess, if necessary, and ask for clarification. Care about their feelings just as much as your own, and express your understanding.

2.4. Pros and Cons of Compassionate Communication

While this approach has considerable benefits, it may not be a panacea for all communication problems. Therefore, analyzing its strengths and limitations is necessary.

On the plus side, Compassionate Communication:

- Fosters Empathy: This method encourages understanding others' perspectives, leading to shared empathy and enhanced relationships.

- Enhances Emotional Intelligence: Understanding and articulating our feelings is key to emotional intelligence development.

- Facilitates Conflict Resolution: By focusing on needs and feelings, conflicts are more likely to be resolved in a peaceful and beneficial manner.

However, the potential limitations might include:

- Prerequisite Understanding: Compassionate communication requires all parties to understand and agree to use this method. If one person adopts this approach and others don't, it may lead to frustration.

- Misconstrued as Confrontational: As it involves expressing feelings directly, some people may feel uncomfortable or view the approach as aggressive.

- Time-Consuming: It might seem cumbersome and time-consuming initially, especially in fast-paced or high-stress environments. But with regular practice, it becomes more natural and effortless.

Despite these challenges, compassionate communication can be a powerful tool for effective and peaceful interactions.

2.5. Compassionate Communication in Action

To effectively embed compassionate communication in your daily life, it's critical to practice regularly. Begin by applying these principles in low-stakes conversations and gradually implement them in more challenging situations. Role-play scenarios, self-reflection exercises, and journaling are some of the techniques that can help hone these skills.

Remember, like any skill, compassionate communication takes time to master. Be kind to yourself as you learn and grow, and always be open to refining and improving your approach.

This compassionate journey promises to improve interpersonal relationships, enhance self-understanding, and contribute towards creating a more peaceful world. With patience, empathy, and practice, you can become a master communicator, fostering compassion and understanding in every conversation you engage in.

Chapter 3. The Science Behind Empathy and Connection

Empathy, often stated as the ability to put oneself in someone else's shoes, is a core facet of human connection. This key human characteristic, driven by our intrinsic social nature, significantly influences our personal relationships, workplace interactions, and collaboration in broader society. Rooted in neuroscience, psychology, and evolutionary biology, the science behind empathy and connection presents a fascinating exploration into the very nature of human behavior and social interaction.

3.1. The Neuroscience of Empathy

Neuroscience has gone a long way in demystifying the complexities of the empathetic response. Whenever we connect with another person's feelings or experiences, certain neural circuits in our brains are activated.

At the heart of empathy lies the mirror neuron system (MNS). Discovered accidentally in the early 1990s by a group of Italian researchers, mirror neurons are special cells in the brain that 'mirror' the actions and emotions of others. That means that observing someone else's actions or emotions activates the same parts of our brain as if we were performing those actions or feeling those emotions ourselves. This 'mirroring' is speculated to be a cornerstone of empathy, enabling us to understand and share others' feelings on a personal level.

Beyond the MNS, scientists tap into another neural path associated with empathy - the anterior insular cortex (AIC) and the anterior cingulate cortex (ACC). The AIC helps us interpret our feelings and those perceived in others, while the ACC plays a role in detecting errors and dealing with conflicting information, which becomes relevant in complex social scenarios.

3.2. The Role of Oxytocin

While discussing the biology of empathy and connection, it's fundamental to mention Oxytocin - a hormone often termed as the 'love' or 'trust' hormone. Oxytocin is released in large amounts during social bonding events like childbirth, breastfeeding, and intimate moments. Its role extends to empathy as well, as it increases our ability to recognize and respond to social cues, encouraging cooperative behaviors and forging social bonds.

3.3. Empathy from a Psychological Perspective

Psychologically, empathy contributes significantly to our ability to maintain social cohesiveness. It equips us with the perspective-taking ability, allowing us to understand and share others' emotional states. There are two primary psychological components of empathy - cognitive empathy, the intellectual ability to comprehend someone else's perspective, and emotional empathy, the capacity to share in another's emotional experience.

Cognitive empathy, rooted in a person's Intelligence Quotient (IQ), forms the basis of our interpersonal problem-solving abilities. In contrast, emotional empathy, more anchored to Emotional Quotient (EQ), enables stronger relationships by creating an emotional resonance between individuals.

3.4. Empathy & Connection: A Societal View

Human beings, by nature, are social creatures. Over millions of years of evolution, we've developed an array of social skills, the keystone being empathy. Without empathy, the social connections that make us human would not exist. Empathy allows individuals to understand and share the feelings of others, enabling cooperation and resolving conflicts—two essential aspects of any thriving society.

When empathetic behaviors promote positive interpersonal interactions and societal cooperation, they culminate into a phenomenon known as social capital. Social capital refers to the networks, norms, and social trust that facilitate coordination and cooperation for mutual benefit. Empathy, therefore, serves as a social glue, allowing for the building of social capital, fostering societal cohesiveness, and promoting collective action.

3.5. Enhancing Empathy: Opportunities & Challenges

While empathy is innate to human beings, research also suggests that it can be cultivated. An individual's ability to empathise can be significantly improved through practices like mindfulness meditation, compassion training, and even through literary fiction, which offers a way to empathetic understanding by inviting readers into the internal lives of characters.

However, enhancing empathy is not without challenges. There is the risk of empathetic distress or compassion fatigue, where repeated or intense experiences of empathy can lead to emotional exhaustion. Another challenge is the empathy gap, where our ability to empathize diminishes with physical or emotional distance. Yet, understanding these challenges offers a starting point for the formation of strategies to address them.

3.6. Conclusion: Towards a More Empathetic Society

Empathy, a core human capacity, plays a crucial role in establishing connections and fostering respect and understanding among individuals. As we navigate our way through the complex socio-political landscape of the 21st century, the need for empathy in communication is more essential than ever before. It is only through the practice of empathetic communication that we can hope to resolve conflicts, promote mutual understanding, and pave the way for a more compassionate society.

Chapter 4. Mindfulness: The Key to Effective Communication

The concept of mindfulness lies at the core of effective communication. Being present in the moment allows us to understand the emotions, desires, and needs that are expressed, sometimes subtly, in our daily interactions. When we deploy mindfulness in our communications, we create a foundation of clarity, understanding, and empathy that can enhance the quality of every interaction we experience.

4.1. Mindfulness: An Introduction

Mindfulness, drawn from Buddhist traditions and increasingly employed in Western psychology, fundamentally refers to the practice of maintaining a moment-by-moment awareness of our thoughts, feelings, bodily sensations, and surrounding environment. Most importantly, mindfulness involves acceptance. This means that we pay attention to our thoughts and feelings without judging them; without believing, for instance, that there's a "right" or "wrong" way to think or feel at a given moment.

When it comes to communication, mindfulness serves as a tool to create a deeper understanding and connection between individuals. It allows us to listen and speak conscientiously, thereby reducing misunderstandings and fostering a sense of empathy and shared experience.

4.2. The Intersection of Mindfulness and Communication

At the intersection of mindfulness and communication is the practice of listening and speaking with full presence and consciousness. Here, we do not merely hear the words spoken by others, but we listen deeply to the emotions, unspoken needs, and ideas that are being conveyed. When we speak, it is not only about expressing our thoughts and emotions, but about doing so with an awareness of our words' impact on others.

When we tread the path of mindful communication, we also go beyond just 'winning' an argument or making our point. Instead, we strive to understand and to be understood, to connect and to enrich our relationships. This act of empathetic, compassionate communication is often the key to resolving conflicts effectively and strengthening bonds.

4.3. The Role of Empathetic Listening in Mindful Communication

Empathetic listening lies at the heart of mindful communication. To truly listen is to strive to understand another person from their perspective. This requires a willingness to set aside our judgments and open our hearts and minds to the speaker's experience.

When you practice empathetic listening, each conversation becomes a potential bridge towards better understanding and a closer connection. By ushering in an era of empathy in our communication practices, we can create stronger, more resilient relationships – be they personal or professional.

4.4. The Power of Respecting Expression

Speaking out responsibly is another vital part of mindful communication. To express ourselves mindfully, we need to be aware of our words, our tone, and the impact they can have on others. Each word we choose, each sentiment we express, carries weight and will have an influence on the course of the conversation and the relationship.

Realizing that we have this power while communicating not only helps us to be more responsible with our expression, but also aids in creating a positive environment in which every voice is heard and respected.

4.5. Mindful Mediation: An Effective Resolution Tool

Mindfulness also plays a significant role in mediation and conflict resolution. When conflicts arise, we often react impulsively, allowing emotions rather than reason to guide our actions. This can escalate conflicts rather than resolve them.

Mindful mediation encourages a shift of focus. It asks us to center our attention on the present moment, on the feelings and needs of all parties involved, rather than on past grievances or future anxieties. It means being aware of our emotions and responses, avoiding blame, and seeking understanding rather than victory.

This approach can transform conflict into an opportunity for growth, allowing disagreements to become platforms for shared understanding and coexistence.

4.6. Practical Techniques for Mindful Communication

Mindful communication can be developed with practice and persistence. Here are some practical techniques that can help you incorporate mindfulness into your everyday communication:

1. Deep Listening: When you listen, give your full attention to the speaker. Avoid planning your response while they are still speaking. Instead, focus on understanding their perspective deeply.

2. Mindful Speaking: Pay attention to your words, your tone, and the effect they have on others. Practice expressing yourself honestly and clearly, while also being kind and considerate.

3. Embrace silence: Don't be afraid of pauses in conversation. Use them to reflect thoughtfully on what has been said and to gauge the appropriate response.

4. Notice Non-Verbal Cues: Be aware of body language, facial expressions, and other non-verbal signals. These can often say more than words.

5. Detached Observation: Practice observing your thoughts and feelings without getting caught up in them. This can help you respond instead of react during conversations.

By integrating these techniques into your life, you can begin a journey towards more mindful, compassionate, and effective communication.

4.7. The Impact of Mindful Communication on Personal Relationships and Workplace Dynamics

Mindful communication has far-reaching impacts on both personal relationships and workplace dynamics. By fostering better understanding, reducing conflicts, and improving the quality of interactions, mindfulness can significantly enhance the emotional wellbeing of individuals and the efficiency of organizations.

On a personal level, mindful communication can lead to deeper, more satisfying relationships. It fosters empathy, patience, and caring – qualities that are the foundation of strong, enduring connections.

In the workplace, mindful communication can reduce stress, improve team harmony, and increase productivity. It does this by promoting a culture of respect and understanding, where employees feel valued and heard.

Whether at home or at work, the mindful way of communicating holds great promise for all who choose to embrace it, promising a better, more harmonious future.

Through mindful and compassionate communication, we can improve our interactions, enhance our relationships, and create a positive change in our world. This future is not just a dream, but a possibility within our grasp if we choose to cultivate mindfulness in our communication. Let's start this journey – one conversation at a time.

Chapter 5. Recognizing Conflict and Understanding Its Roots

Conflict is as old as humanity itself. Since time immemorial, humans have engaged in disputes and struggles for survival, dominance, and resolve differences. Conflict, at its core, is a discord of action, direction, or idea between two or more parties. It surrounds us in various forms and intensities, existing potentially in every human relationship.

5.1. Understanding Conflict

It's critical to understand that conflict should neither be vilified nor celebrated; instead, it must be acknowledged, explored, and leveraged constructively. Conflict isn't inherently negative, despite its common connotation as 'bad'. It can often initiate progress, discovery, learning, and growth. However, if unresolved, it can spiral into harmful and destructive behavior, affecting personal health, relationships, and social harmony.

Paradoxically, conflict avoidance, seen as a 'peaceful strategy,' can lead to seething resentments, misunderstandings, and disengagement over time. Thus, it becomes essential to recognize conflict not as a detrimental occurrence but as an opportunity for potential growth and transformation.

The origin of a conflict lies in the 'perceived' incompatibility of goals, values, expectations, or behaviors. It is fueled by emotions such as frustration, anger, fear, and hurt, creating barriers, triggering reactions, and often leading individuals on a path of blame and retaliation. Thus, understanding the nature and roots of conflict is the first step towards mindful conflict resolution.

5.2. Recognizing Conflict: Signs and Indicators

Recognizing conflict involves being aware of indications that suggest a discord exists. These indications often manifest as:

- Emotional signs: Passive aggression, resentment, defensiveness, anger, fear, heightened stress, and anxiety.

- Behavioral signs: Withdrawal, avoidance, confrontational interactions, decreased productivity, and changes in work or personal habits.

- Communication signs: Increased miscommunication, increased use of negative language, heated arguments, personal attacks, and blame-shifting.

Recognizing these signs is the first step in addressing a conflict. Ignoring or downplaying these indications often exacerbates the situation. Openly acknowledging these signs encourages the parties involved to start a dialogue aiming for resolution.

5.3. The Roots of Conflict

Diverse roots underpin conflicts, each complex and deeply intertwined with the others. Identifying these origins allows for an in-depth understanding of the conflict, paving the way for effective resolutions.

5.3.1. Difference in Goals and Values

Conflicts often arise when the values or goals of the individuals or groups involved do not align. At the personal level, this can manifest as disagreements on individual priorities or lifestyles. In the workplace, conflict can surface due to clashing visions or strategies among team members.

5.3.2. Resource Scarcity

Limited resources, whether tangible like money, time, and physical assets, or intangible like recognition and status, often create conflicts by triggering competition. The perceived scarcity makes individuals or groups vie for the same, leading to a struggle.

5.3.3. Miscommunication or Misunderstanding

Miscommunication or misunderstanding is another common root of conflict. Misinterpretation of information or misperception of an individual's action, intent, or words can create discord, leading to conflict.

5.3.4. Power Dynamics

Conflicts often stem from struggle for control or power, especially in hierarchical environments. This could range from personal relationships to global political dynamics. Unequal power distribution often leads to conflicts as parties feel oppressed or suppressed.

5.3.5. Past Resentments

Unresolved past conflicts or resentments could also be a fertile ground for ongoing conflicts. These lingering grudges often magnify minor disagreements, leading to larger conflicts.

5.4. Role of Perception and Emotion in Conflict

Perceptions and emotions significantly influence conflicts. Perception is reality in conflict scenarios—the way you perceive the conflict shapes your emotional response and behavior during the engagement.

For instance, if you perceive a disagreement as an attack, you are likely to react defensively, further escalating the conflict. However, if you perceive the same disagreement as a chance to learn and grow, your response will be constructive, focusing on resolution and understanding.

Similarly, emotions play a significant role in conflicts. When feelings like anger, fear, or hurt surface, they often cloud judgement, leading to impulsive or reactive behavior. Understanding that emotional reactions are normal during conflicts, but not always helpful, can aid in managing conflicts better.

5.5. Conclusion

In conclusion, understanding and recognizing conflict, as well as understanding its roots, is critical for effective conflict resolution. Conflict is not inherently negative; it is merely an indicator of a perceived incompatibility that needs addressing. Recognizing the signs and indicators is the first step in conflict resolution, followed by understanding the conflict's roots, which can span from differences in values to power dynamics. Perception and emotional response are key players in shaping conflicts and can significantly influence the resolution process.

Learning to recognize conflict and its roots is a vital skill in our personal and professional lives. It allows us to respond to conflicts mindfully, compassionately, and constructively, fostering more harmonious relationships and environments. This understanding, coupled with the art of empathetic listening and respectful expression, can dramatically shift our approach to dealing with conflicts, making us architects of peace and harmony in our spheres of influence.

Chapter 6. Harnessing Emotion: Strategies for Emotional Self-Regulation

In developing emotionally intelligent communication, managing our own emotional reactions is paramount. Emotional self-regulation, a part of emotional intelligence, refers to our ability to manage disruptive emotions effectively and bring our best selves to our interactions. This chapter will explore various strategies through which this can be achieved.

6.1. Understanding Emotional Triggers

Our emotional responses are often precipitated by certain events or circumstances, also known as triggers. Identifying these emotional triggers is the first step towards effective self-regulation. The triggers could be an individual, a situation or a combination of both. Emotional journaling can help in recognizing these triggers.

To begin with, take note of each time you experience a strong emotion. Write down the situation, people involved, and your immediate emotional response. Over time, patterns may emerge; recurring events or particular individuals may always spark a specific emotion in you. Recognizing these patterns is the key to controlling your emotional reactions substantively.

6.2. The Power of Pause

A fundamental strategy for emotional self-regulation is mastering the power of bit - to pause and think before reacting. This pause gives us the chance to process the event and our initial emotional response objectively, allowing us to choose a more productive response.

The power of pause can be exercised through conscious practice. When you identify a trigger, train yourself to take a momentary break before reacting. During this break, engage in deep breathing, count to ten, or simply step away temporarily from the situation.

6.3. Mindfulness and Emotional Self-regulation

Mindfulness takes the power of pause a step further - it encourages present moment awareness. By focusing on our thoughts, feelings, and physical sensations, we can recognize our emotions as they arise, without immediately reacting to them.

A simple way to start mindfulness practice is through mindful breathing. When something triggers a strong emotion, bring your focus to your breath for a few moments. Pay attention as the breath enters and leaves your body. This deliberate focus can diffuse emotional intensity and provide the clarity required for effective response.

Practicing mindfulness on an everyday basis can help increase emotional awareness and regulate responses even before the emotions are full-blown, reducing emotional havoc in communication.

6.4. Cognitive Reappraisal Strategy

Cognitive reappraisal involves changing our interpretation of emotion-eliciting situations. It starts with accepting that our emotions are not directly caused by events, but by how we perceive these events. By changing our perspective or reframing the event, we can modify our emotional response.

For instance, consider a colleague criticizing your project. Rather than allowing anger to take control, reframe the criticism as an opportunity to improve your work. This cognitive reappraisal can transform a potentially negative interaction into a productive conversation.

6.5. Body Regulation Techniques

Our physical state can impact our emotional state. Techniques such as deep breathing, progressive muscle relaxation, and regular exercise can regulate emotional balance effectively.

Deep breathing can quickly calm a reactive state of mind. In stressful situations, take deep, slow breaths. Focus on the sensation of air entering and leaving your lungs. This can act as an instant emotional regulator.

Progressive muscle relaxation involves tensing and then releasing different muscle groups in your body, starting from your toes and working your way up to your head. This method can help ease tension caused by emotional stress.

Lastly, regular exercise has been found to have long-term positive effects on emotional self-regulation. Physical activity releases endorphins, chemicals in the brain that act as natural mood lifters. Exercise also promotes better sleep and boosts self-esteem, enhancing overall emotional health.

Understanding, identifying, and managing emotions aren't skills acquired overnight. It's a journey of self-discovery and growth. Conscious efforts to utilize the power of pause, integrate mindfulness into your life, use cognitive reappraisal strategies, and adopt body regulation techniques can significantly enhance your ability to regulate emotions. This journey will transform the way you communicate, enhancing interpersonal relationships, and fostering compassionate communication.

Chapter 7. Compassionate Listening: The Silent Impact

Listening is an integral part of communication, but effective listening goes far beyond merely hearing the words spoken by another. It requires understanding, attention, empathy, and compassion. This chapter dives deep into the concept of compassionate listening - listening with an intent to understand rather than to respond, and with an open mind and heart to the feelings, perspectives, and experiences of the one speaking.

7.1. Understanding Compassionate Listening

At its core, compassionate listening is an act of empathy in which one seeks to genuinely understand and connect with another person's experiences. To master this skill requires a myriad understanding of the speaker's perspectives and an openness to their emotions and experiences. It's about stepping into their shoes, feeling their emotions, and perceiving their viewpoint without judgment or criticism.

Compared to regular listening, which often involves passively receiving information, compassionate listening takes a proactive stance. It urges the listener to delve deeper into the speaker's experiences, peel back the layers of their emotional state, and grasp the underlying messages often concealed between lines.

7.2. The Power of Silence

In compassionate listening, silence is not a void but a powerful tool. It allows the listener to process what is being shared, and provides the speaker space to reflect and express themselves fully.

Often, we tend to fill silence with words, viewing it as a sign of discomfort. However, in compassionate listening, silence is cherished. It allows the listener to absorb the weight of the speaker's words, and provides a serene atmosphere for the speaker to divulge their feelings without feeling rushed or judged.

It's worth noting that silence mustn't be confused with withdrawal or disinterest. An appropriate marker of compassionate listening in silence is an engaged body language, expressive eyes, and responsive non-verbal cues like nodding and maintaining eye contact.

7.3. Empathy over Sympathy

Compassionate listening thrives on empathy rather than sympathy. While sympathy can come across as pity or feeling sorry for someone, empathy calls for a deeper connection with the speaker's experiences. It's about feeling 'with' them rather than feeling 'for' them.

When listening with empathy, the listener doesn't merely acknowledge the speaker's emotions; they strive to sense their intensity, understand their origin, and respect their validity. They aim to appreciate the speaker's feelings authentically without trying to alter, negate, or solve them.

7.4. Moving Beyond Biases

In our lives, we all carry perceptions, beliefs, and biases that influence how we interpret what we hear. Compassionate listening requires keeping these biases in check, allowing the speaker's narrative to come forth unfiltered.

This concept of 'bracketing' – setting aside personal judgments and biases, is crucial in compassionate listening. It enables the listener to fully engage with the speaker's emotions and ideas as they are, without coloring them with their perspective.

The practice of bracketing isn't about denying one's beliefs or biases but recognizing them and temporarily dissociating from them while listening compassionately. It's about the listener surrendering their role as the 'knower' and assuming the role of a 'learner', absorbing the speaker's experiences and emotions in their raw, true form.

7.5. Techniques for Compassionate Listening

Active compassionate listening isn't accidental: it requires conscious effort and practice. Several techniques aid in fostering this unique communication skill.

1. Paraphrasing: Reflecting what the speaker says in your own words confirms understanding and sends a signal that you're attentive.

2. Reflection of feelings: Identifying and stating the speaker's emotions demonstrates empathy and builds trust.

3. Clarification: Asking open-ended questions helps in gaining a deeper understanding of the speaker's experience and feelings.

4. Summarization: Giving a comprehensive summary of what has been shared verifies understanding, and helps the speaker feel heard and understood.

7.6. Compassionate Listening in Conflict Resolution

In conflict situations, compassionate listening serves as a powerful peacemaking tool. It aids in diffusing tension, fostering understanding, and building bridges of connection between conflicting parties.

Through the practice of compassionate listening, each party has the opportunity to express their feelings, perspectives, and needs openly without fear of judgment or interruption. This process catalyzes healing, validating their experiences whilst opening avenues for constructive dialogue and peaceful resolution of the conflict.

Adopting compassionate listening in conflicts reframes them as opportunities for growth and connection, moving beyond the damaging scope of win or lose towards win-win solutions based on mutual respect and understanding.

7.7. The Lifelong Journey of Compassionate Listening

Compassionate listening is not a skill that is mastered overnight but a lifelong journey. It requires continuous practice, self-reflection, and iteration. It calls for a shift in mindset, wherein listening is perceived not just as an act of receiving information but as a path towards understanding, empathy, and connection.

Cultivating compassionate listening offers numerous benefits. Besides fostering stronger relationships and healthy conflict resolution, it empowers individuals to be more present, mindful, and receptive in their interactions with others. It teaches us to value the perspectives and emotions of others just as we value our own.

In conclusion, while words have the power to connect us, it is our silent compassion, our ability to listen deeply to others, that truly brings us together. Practicing compassionate listening can bring a sea of positive change to our relationships, workplaces, and communities, shaping a more empathetic and understanding world.

Thus, embark on this journey of mastering compassionate listening, for it's not just about becoming better communicators, but more compassionate and understanding human beings.

Chapter 8. Effective Techniques for Expressing Empathy

Effective communication cannot occur without empathy in the mix. Empathy is all about understanding and sharing another person's feelings, essentially putting yourself in their shoes. The following techniques will guide you to successfully express empathy in your daily interactions.

8.1. The Power of Active Listening

Active listening is a cornerstone of empathetic communication. This practice requires you to fully concentrate, understand, respond, and then remember what is being said. Unlike passive listening, active listening involves participating in the conversation, offering responses when necessary, and demonstrating that you're engaged.

To start, let the other person speak without interruption. Take care not to formulate your responses while they're talking - the goal is to hear them. Respond with short, encouraging prompts like "Go on" or "I understand," to show that you are keeping up with the conversation. Maintain eye contact, nod occasionally, and rephrase what they've said to show comprehension. Remember, your aim is to understand, not necessarily to agree!

8.2. Understanding Non-Verbal Communication

Non-verbal cues play an essential role in expressing empathy. They provide context and can help convey emotions without saying a word. Understanding these cues can help you connect on a deeper level with the speaker.

Watch out for body language, facial expressions, and tone of voice. A furrowed brow, crossed arms, a shaky voice - all these could signal how the speaker is feeling. Mirror their body language subtly to convey that you're in tune with them.

8.3. Open-Ended Questions

Expressing empathy involves not just understanding the specific details the speaker shares, but the entire context surrounding their feelings and situation. Utilize open-ended questions to help the speaker disclose deeper emotions and experiences.

Start your queries with "how," "what," "when," or "why." Use sensitive phrasing such as, "Can you tell me more about...", or "How did that make you feel?" This shows not only that you are engaged, but also interested in understanding their perspective.

8.4. Expressing Empathy through Words

We often underestimate the power of words. The language we use has the potential to demonstrate compassion in both personal and professional contexts. Nurturing a wide emotional vocabulary allows us to better encapsulate feelings, thus offering appropriate empathetic responses.

Consider phrases like, "I'm here for you," "That must have been hard for you," or simply "I understand your situation." They indicate a nonjudgmental approach and willingness to listen.

8.5. The Art of Validation

The act of validation is simply recognizing and expressing understanding of someone else's feelings. It doesn't necessarily mean you agree with the person or their decisions, but rather that you empathize with their emotions or their situation.

Clear communication is crucial in validation. A simple phrase like "I understand why you feel that way" can increase the other person's comfort and willingness to express themselves more openly. This reinforces trust, connection, and mutual respect.

8.6. Effective Reflective Listening

Reflective listening is a step further from active listening. It requires you to reflect the speaker's emotions back to them. Upsetting feelings can be diffuse and overwhelming; by reflecting these emotions back with succinct language, you can help people better understand and manage their feelings.

This can translate to statements such as, "It sounds like you're really overwhelmed with this," or "It seems like you're really excited about this opportunity." Reflective listening requires you to truly grasp the emotion behind the words of the speaker.

8.7. Emotional Intelligence: Your X-Factor

Your ability to express empathy is greatly enhanced by emotional intelligence. Emotional intelligence is the capacity to be aware of, control, and express your emotions, and to handle interpersonal relationships judiciously and empathetically.

Developing emotional intelligence involves acknowledging your own emotions, and managing them in a constructive way. It also means recognizing emotions in others, and understanding the effect of your actions and words on those around you. By nurturing emotional intelligence, you allow for a more profound and meaningful expression of empathy.

8.8. Building Empathy through Practice

Lastly, remember empathy is like a muscle - it needs to be exercised and inevitably grows stronger with use. By intentionally practicing these techniques, you can cultivate a more empathetic communication style.

Through active listening, understanding non-verbal cues, posing open-ended questions, and using empathetic language you can convey empathy. Validate the speaker's emotions, utilize reflective listening, and harness emotional intelligence. With time, these techniques will become a natural part of your communication style, making your interactions more meaningful, receptive, and empathetic.

Empathy is a powerful tool in our interpersonal connections. It allows us to understand each other better, build strong relationships, and creates a more compassionate world. By applying these techniques, we pave the road for understanding, harmony, and empathy to thrive - one conversation at a time.

Remember, expressing empathy is not a transactional act, but a transformational journey that builds understanding, trust, and connection. And through this, we can all contribute to making the world a more compassionate place.

Chapter 9. Navigating Difficult Conversations with Mindfulness

Having a difficult conversation is something many of us typically avoid. Whether it's a disagreement with a coworker or facing a personal confrontation, a lot of us feel unequipped to navigate these rough waters. However, is it possible to have a mindful approach that fosters understanding and empathy throughout this process? The answer is a resounding yes. This section will take you through a deep dive into the nuances of navigating difficult conversations with mindfulness.

9.1. Understanding Mindfulness in Communication

To begin with, it's imperative to grasp the concept of mindfulness in the context of communication. Mindfulness is about being present in the moment without judgment. It's about fully engaging in what is happening right now, rather than being caught up in past regrets or future anxieties. In conversations, being mindful can help us respond thoughtfully rather than react hastily.

In a difficult conversation, your focus should be on what is being expressed and how it's being communicated. This requires attentively listening, maintaining open body language, and being in tune with the emotions and nuances of the dialogue. Resisting the urge to plan your responses while still listening is crucial to demonstrating active mindfulness.

9.2. Managing Your Reactions

When stressful situations arise, our bodies naturally go into 'fight or flight' mode. This biological reaction can cloud our judgment, resulting in rash decisions or harsh words that could escalate the situation. Mindfulness can enable us to manage this better - it requires conscious and sympathetic acknowledgment of our feelings, which can help us calm down and think more clearly.

Start by identifying your emotional responses - are you feeling defensive, frustrated, or anxious? Once recognized, allow yourself to experience these feelings without condemning or denying them. Remember, it's okay to feel these emotions. Understanding them and managing your reactions can prevent the conversation from spiraling out of control.

9.3. Active Listening and Empathetic Responding

Genuine listening provides a foundation for dialogue. It allows us to gain insight into the other person's perspective and better understand the situation at hand. Mindfulness helps us be active listeners without mentally formulating responses or feeling reactive. Empathetic responding is the next step, representing our feelings and thoughts based on what we've carefully listened to, without projecting blame or judgment.

A helpful technique here could be 'reflective responding', in which you mirror back what you understood from the speaker's words. For instance, you might say, "What I'm hearing is that you felt upset when..." Accurate reflective responding demonstrates understanding and has the potential to temper heated moments, making way for resolution.

9.4. Responding with Respect and Integrity

Mindful communication requires us to respond with respect and integrity, especially during difficult interactions. Even when challenging someone's viewpoint, it is essential to maintain respect for their feelings and thoughts. Mindfulness enables this by encouraging us to express ourselves honestly and plainly, without the intention to harm or demean.

The 'I statement' technique can be applied here. The idea is to center your expressions on your own sentiments instead of focusing on the other individual's actions. For example, "I feel upset when you interrupt me during meetings," promotes dialogue and mutual comprehension rather than, "You always interrupt me."

9.5. The Role of Mindful Pauses

Occasionally, the most effective response is silence. Pausing and taking a few deep breaths, especially during emotionally fraught moments in a conversation, can help you gather your thoughts and approach the next part of the discussion with mindfulness and clarity. These 'mindful pauses' support the regulation of emotional responses, leading to better communication.

9.6. The Importance of Forgiveness and Letting Go

Finally, a critical aspect of navigating difficult conversations with mindfulness is the practice of forgiveness and the ability to let go. Holding onto resentment is likely to influence future discussions negatively, leading to further conflict. Instead, we should aim for resolution and understanding, knowing that people can make mistakes and that holding onto grudges benefits nobody.

Forgiveness is not about forgetting, it's about accepting what has transpired, learning the lesson, and anticipating a better future. This mindset fosters an atmosphere of compassion and empathy in our communications, facilitating healing and promoting stronger relationships.

In conclusion, difficult conversations are an inevitable part of our lives. However, by integrating mindfulness into our communication toolkit, we can navigate these complexities more effectively, building a universe of understanding, empathy, and harmony one conversation at a time. These skills not only help in managing conflicts but also enrich our experiences and growth as emotionally intelligent individuals.

Chapter 10. Case Studies of Mindful Conflict Resolution

To fully explore the practice and impacts of mindful conflict resolution, we will delve into three illuminating case studies. These will cover a diverse range of scenarios: a tense family disagreement, a workplace power struggle, and a town hall meeting turned heated debate. Each will shed light on how mindful conflict resolution techniques can transform even the most complicated disputes into powerful opportunities for growth and connection.

10.1. Case Study 1: The Family Misunderstanding

There existed a family of four: Amanda, the mother, Ben, the father, Charlie, the elder son, and Daisy, the younger daughter. All shared a loving bond, but a little misunderstanding triggered an unexpected conflict.

Over dinner, Charlie mentions his plans to drop out of college to start his entrepreneurial journey. His revelation ignites an immediate reaction from his parents, fueled by concerns about his future and the risk he might be taking. Daisy, feeling Charlie's distress but not wanting to escalate the situation, stays silent.

Through the lens of mindful conflict resolution, let's explore how the situation could have unfolded differently.

Amanda, instead of reacting immediately with anger and concern for Charlie's future, could have paused. In that pause, she would make space for empathy, trying to understand her son's perspective. Recognizing the apprehension in his voice, she might say, "I can see you've given this a lot of thought, Charlie. It sounds like this is important to you."

Similarly, Ben, instead of expressing disappointment indirectly, could have been more open and honest about his feelings. He could have said, "I feel scared because your security matters to me. Can we discuss this in more detail?"

Daisy, instead of remaining silent, might have used this opportunity to mediate the conversation, ensuring that everyone's concerns and emotions are acknowledged fairly. She could voice her own feelings and encourage others to do the same.

10.2. Case Study 2: The Workplace Power Struggle

Surprisingly, offices can be war zones, too! There were two colleagues - Emily and Frances - working in a corporate setting. They shared the same roles but harbored competitive attitudes towards each other. This competitiveness soon turned into a series of conflicts.

Imagine if Emily, instead of viewing Frances as a rival, saw her as a fellow team member. A shift from "competition" to "collaboration" could have drastically changed the contours of their relationship. By expressing genuine respect for Frances's abilities, Emily could foster a more positive and congenial work environment.

Concurrently, Frances, feeling vied against by Emily, may lash out publicly. However, mindful conflict resolution suggests acknowledging her feelings of being threatened and finding constructive ways to express them. Instead of reacting impulsively, she could address the issue privately with Emily, stating her observations and feelings, "Emily, I noticed we have been at odds lately. I am feeling quite stressed about it. Can we talk about how we can work better together?"

Investing in empathetic listening and respectful expression, both parties could reach a resolution leading to a more harmonious and productive workspace.

10.3. Case Study 3: The Town Hall Meeting

In a small coastal town, the governing body proposed constructing a new pier. Some residents were thrilled about the idea as it could boost the town's economy via tourism. However, other citizens view this development as a potential environmental threat.

In one town hall meeting, the clash of different opinions created a turbulent atmosphere filled with anger and resentment. Emotions ran high, and productive conversation was nowhere on the horizon.

With mindful conflict resolution, a different approach could have been taken. The town mayor, as a neutral figurehead, could have allowed each resident to speak without interruption, ensuring everyone feels heard and respected. He could have practiced empathetic listening, acknowledging the feelings present in the room.

After everyone has shared their perspectives, the meeting could turn towards collaboration, openly discussing potential solutions that address both economic and environmental concerns. Soliciting ideas from citizens about implementation strategies and safety measures could have turned conflict into cooperation.

Through these case studies, we see how mindful conflict resolution techniques can change the texture of disagreements and misunderstandings. By making room for empathy, honing the skill of active listening, and respectful expression, we can transform our interactions, forging deeper connections and fostering harmony.

These accounts provide evidence of the effectiveness of this approach, offering insights and lessons that readers can apply to conflicts they may face in their own lives. They cement the idea that embracing these compassionate communication strategies can yield positive results, leading to more rewarding personal relationships, improved workplace dynamics, and heightened community cooperation.

Chapter 11. Embodying Compassionate Communication: Your Path Forward

Compassionate communication, sometimes referred to as 'Nonviolent Communication', is a language of empathy, honesty, and respect that promotes harmonious relations among individuals. It provides us with strategies to manage our interactions, which can lead to profound connections and effective resolutions to conflicts. Embodied compassionate communication is more than a mere model of communication; it is a way to enrich our life experiences and build stronger, more understanding connections with others.

11.1. The Foundation of Compassionate Communication

In order to embrace compassionate communication, one must first understand its foundation, which is based on non-judgmental presence, empathy, and genuine understanding. It means to listen with full attention and intent to connect rather than debate, criticize, or instruct. With each interaction, we are given the opportunity to foster deeper relationships, build mutual respect, and encourage positive dialogue.

Compassionate communication requires us to let go of our preconceived notions and habitual responses. Instead of focusing on who is right or wrong, we strive to recognize and respect each other's feelings and experiences. This can lead to a state of mutual understanding and shared reality, facilitating more effective conflict resolution.

11.2. Tools for Compassionate Communication

Embodying compassionate communication also involves mastering a set of tools and techniques. Here are some of them:

1. Active Listening: This involves fully focusing on the speaker, seeking to understand their feelings and needs, and maintaining an open, non-judgmental mindset.

2. Non-Violent Expression: This implies conveying your thoughts and feelings respectfully, without blaming or attacking. It stresses the importance of using "I" statements (example: "I feel upset...") instead of "you" statements (example: "you make me upset...").

3. Emotional Intelligence: This aids in recognizing and managing your own emotions and the emotions of others. It facilitates better understanding and mutual respect.

4. Mindfulness: This stresses being present in the moment rather than ruminating on the past or worrying about the future. It enables a deeper connection between communicators.

5. Conflict Resolution Skills: These are strategies to diffuse tension and arrive at a mutually agreeable solution, which includes negotiation, mediation, compromise, and reconciliation.

11.3. Cultivating Empathy in Communication

Empathy lies at the heart of compassionate communication. It involves stepping into the shoes of another person to understand their emotions and perspectives. When we communicate with empathy, we validate others' feelings, making them feel understood and valued.

Ways to cultivate empathy in communication include effective listening, being present, acknowledging feelings without judgment, mirroring emotions to show understanding, and expressing genuine interest and curiosity about the person's experience.

Empathy not only fosters more compassionate and meaningful interactions but also helps defuse potential conflict situations. When people feel heard and understood, they are more likely to engage in constructive discussions instead of heated arguments.

11.4. Transforming Your Personal Relationships with Compassionate Communication

Your journey towards embodying compassionate communication can have a profound impact on your personal relationships. This approach can foster deeper connections with family members, friends, and romantic partners by promoting mutual understanding, reducing conflict, and boosting your capacity for intimacy.

There are several techniques through which this transformation can happen. One is the practice of active listening, which involves fully focusing on the other person and striving to understand their emotional state. Also, understanding that everyone has the right to their feelings and opinions, and respecting those, even in disagreement.

Mindfulness also plays a crucial role as it helps us stay present in the moment and fosters deeper connections. The practice of mindful communication where we strive to be present, fully engaged and receptive to what the other person is saying can make a significant positive impact.

11.5. Managing Workplace Dynamics through Compassionate Communication

The influence of compassionate communication extends well beyond personal relationships and into the professional sphere. It can help foster a harmonious environment, enhanced team collaboration, increased productivity, and reduced conflict at the workplace.

Leaders can use compassionate communication to convey their expectations clearly, provide constructive feedback, and inspire their team. For employees, this form of communication can remind others that they are heard, valued, and understood, thus contributing to happy, productive, and cohesive teams.

In workplace conflicts, compassionate communication helps address the core issues in a respectful and understanding manner. By focusing on the needs and feelings of all parties involved, it facilitates mutual understanding and comes up with solutions that account for everyone's needs.

11.6. Conclusion: Marching Towards a Compassionate Society

Compassionate communication can truly become a path forward for humanity. It offers us a powerful tool to build harmony, understanding, and mutual respect in our societies. It emphasizes the recognition of our shared humanity and the need for kindness and compassion in our interactions.

As we embody compassionate communication in our lives, we not only transform our personal relationships and professional dynamics but also contribute to a more compassionate society. It yields benefits of harmony, cooperation, and mutual respect.

So, let's embark on this journey together, fostering empathy, understanding, and harmony. This is our path forward to a stronger, more compassionate world—one conversation at a time. Remember, every conversation is a new opportunity to practice and embody compassionate communication.